How to Write Your Kindle Book and Sell It On Amazon

Get Your Ideas Published and Make Money Doing It!

by

Tamar Clevenger

Tamar Clevenger

ISBN: **1517387302**

ISBN-13: **978-1517387303**

DEDICATION

This book is dedicated to Renee M. Pittman, William Forstchen, Mark M. Rich and all of the authors who wrote ebooks that inspired and motivated me. This book is also dedicated to my beautiful daughter, who I miss and love very much.

I believe that we all have a voice, and that voice deserves to be heard. Thank you all for motivating me to write this work.

Tamar Clevenger

Preface

If you have the desire to write a book and publish it on Amazon, this step-by-step guide will help you navigate the way. "How to Write Your Kindle Book and Publish It on Amazon" logically walks the reader through the creative steps of identifying a concept, turning the concept into a solid topic and publishing your work both as a paperback and an ebook.

Tamar's style is light, airy, engaging and easy to follow – and humorous at times. Even if you have never written an article or book in the past, this book will take you through the process, answering any questions you may have along the way. For those new to self-publishing, this book pulls back the veil of mystery to reveal tools and platforms that will facilitate getting your book published fast.

If you have a couple of hours to spare, grab a cup of coffee and read this book today. Tamar motivates and inspires while walking you through the entire adventure of authoring and self-publishing your future bestseller.

Tamar Clevenger

TABLE OF CONTENTS

CHAPTER 1: INTRODUCTION

The idea has been churning inside you for quite a while - that burning desire to put your creative thoughts to paper never leaves you but you keep making excuses. You're too busy; there are just not enough hours in the day. Your family, friends, co-workers, (insert group here) need you and you just can't take the time to sit down and write that book. You know that you have something relevant and interesting to share with the public, but you just haven't taken the steps to produce that tome that resides within you.

However, the tide is changing – today! You have now committed yourself to your goal of writing that book by taking the time to reading this one! The time is NOW to start that masterpiece you have been putting off forever. Stop procrastinating! Find out how to get your voice heard and make some money doing so.

Why Now?

Instead of "Why Now?" how about we rephrase the question as "Why NOT Now?" The time that it takes to write your book will pass anyway, whether you have a book to show for it or not. You will be one year older next year. You will still be trying to pay the bills and keep your head above water. Your days are not very likely to get less busy as the time goes on. So, I ask again, why NOT commit to making NOW the time to get your thoughts down on paper?

You <u>CAN</u> carve out a few hours per day to contribute to your dream - you <u>NEED</u> to do it. If you have that driving force inside you - that voice that needs to be heard - your well-being depends on making it happen. Also, the world needs to hear what you have to say! No matter how busy your days are, you can set aside some time to move toward your ultimate goal of writing and publishing your opus. The keys to reaching your goal are 1.) To get organized, and 2.) To stay focused. By getting organized and staying focused on your goal, you may just be surprised how the book seems to magically write itself! With all that said, let's get started...

This book provides step-by-step, easy to follow instructions for getting your book written and published in paperback format. If you follow the instructions documented here, there is absolutely no doubt that you will become a published author by the time you reach the end of the process. The process can take a week or a year; depending on how committed you are to the goal. The more you write, the more sheer momentum will propel you forward toward completion. Just keep moving – one step at a time. After all, you know the old adage: The journey of 1000 miles begins with one step. Take that step.

Image courtesy of KeepCalm-o-Matic

The Digital Revolution

The ebook's time has arrived. Digital books provide readers with convenience and speed. No more waiting for the book to arrive in the mail or trekking to the nearest bookstore to pour over paperbacks and hard covers, hoping to find content of interest. Today, with just a few clicks, readers can sample a book, read reviews, order the book and have it delivered to their mobile device or computer – all in a matter of about 5 minutes. Is it any wonder why the popularity of ebooks grows steadily over time?

Established publishing houses report a dramatic increase in the sales of digital books over the past 5 years. Random House reported in 2012 that electronic content represented approximately 20% of their total sales. That number in 2015 has risen to over 30%. The leader of the pack in the ebook market is Amazon Kindle. Kindle reading is so popular that Kindle ebook sales now represent nearly 20% of all book sales in the US! The digital revolution is well underway and Amazon is leading the herd.

So, what does this all mean for authors? It means that the time has never been better to write your book and self-publish in digital form on an electronic platform. The tools are available and most of the bugs have been eliminated from the process, so take advantage of these fantastic opportunities afforded to authors in the 21st century and publish your book as an ebook, too! Just keep reading. In this book, we'll cover how to self-publish your book in paperback and ebook format – at the same time!

Why Amazon?

Amazon is clearly the Big Dog, the company at the forefront of the digital publishing revolution. Amazon now sells more Kindle books than paperbacks and hard cover books combined! Forbes reported in 2014 the annual revenue from Amazon book sales topped $5.25 Billion (that's Billion with a "B") per year – and books only represent only 7% of Amazon's total sales. Amazon Kindle ebooks account for about 65% of all digital books sold, with Barnes and Noble and Apple claiming the remaining 35 % of global sales.

Amazon is amazing. I'm a huge fan of Amazon for my own personal purchases, from tools to computer gear. However, Amazon was originally founded as a site that primarily sold books and media. The company has all but perfected the ecommerce business model. But wait, there's more! Amazon has established an amazingly efficient platform for self-publishing. This platform is named CreateSpace.

From the CreateSpace web application, you can format, design, publish and market your work. Additionally, CreateSpace provides an accounting system to ensure that authors are paid royalties for their work. Though some limitations exist with CreateSpace, the platform is a Godsend to authors seeking to make their work available without the backing of a publishing house. For authors who don't necessarily want to publish in print, those who prefer to publish their content in ebook form only, the Amazon Kindle Direct platform accommodates this option. KDP is integrated with CreateSpace, so authors still have the account management and marketing tools available at their fingertips. More about CreateSpace and KDP will be revealed in later chapters. Just know for now that Amazon is not the only game in town for self-publishing authors, however, it really is your best option.

Tamar Clevenger

CHAPTER 2: BEFORE SITTING DOWN TO WRITE

First Things First

Before you sit down to write your first word, invest a little time getting organized and focused. The first order of business is to determine a concept for your work. Once you have a concept in mind, your unconscious brain tends to focus on the concept, gleaning information from your day-to-day life that you probably wouldn't notice otherwise. You set a course when you begin to ponder a concept.

The task of identifying your concept is not as difficult as it may seem at first glance. As a writer, you probably find yourself deriving motivation and ideas from other writers. If you are like me, reading other authors' writings probably remind you of all the things you have to say. You can capitalize on this impulse to generate a solid, relevant and timely concept for your book.

Image courtesy of DIYAuthor.com

Time Is Of the Essence

No matter what topics you write about, whether you are a fiction or non-fiction writer, one of the keys to attracting readers to your work is to provide them with relevant, timely content. First, you will need to identify trends in book sales to determine which topics are hot and which are not. For example, How To books (ironically, just like this one) are a hot commodity in the non-fiction genre – particularly books that show the reader how she can make money. Funny how that works out, right? Regardless of your genre, finding out what is selling is one way to set a course to find the concept for your brilliant bestseller.

Market Research for Writers

One of the most useful tools for writers searching for a new topic is the Amazon Bestsellers list. Well technically, Amazon publishes several Bestseller lists, but we are mainly interested in the Bestselling Books list. This list has been very fruitful for many writers looking for a fresh, new concept to write about. Another interesting list I like to keep up with is the Amazon Hot New Releases list – if only just to stay current with what the competition is doing.

Amazon Bestsellers List

Carefully peruse the Amazon Bestsellers list and take note of the most popular reads. Note that, in general, most books on the bestseller list at any given time are fiction. Fiction seems to sell better than non-fiction on Amazon. So, if you are struggling to decide between writing that novel that has always been churning inside you, or writing a How To book instructing readers how to master one of your many talents, the data leans toward the novel. In my case, I am just not a creative writer. Yes, I have written some creative pieces, but as a former academic, my talents tend to lie solely in the non-fiction realm.

While studying the Bestsellers list, focus on the categories that are trending. In the non-fiction genre, dieting and weight loss titles, as well as business and entrepreneurial books, tend to be particularly hot topics. Note that the list is updated every hour, so the research you do on one day will differ if you try to replicate it the next day – or hour. Plan to do your concept market research in one sitting to avoid confusion. The time required to complete this exercise entirely depends on you. Many authors spend weeks researching topics and titles. Others seem to have an instinct for quickly conceptualizing trending topics and identifying interesting titles. For this book, I had an idea going into the exercise about my genre and general topic. It was simply a matter of confirming what I already suspected with regards to reader interest.

Pay particular attention to the structure and content of the bestselling titles and subtitles in the list. Wording of titles matters more than you can imagine for digital content. You always want to give your book a catchy title that makes the reader want to dive in, but during this exercise, take note of the titles that draw you in. When you find a book that you want to buy and read on the spot, there's your sign. Additionally, pay attention to the subtitles of the books that interest you. In an Amazon search, interesting titles and subtitles are crucial for coaxing the reader to dig deeper by clicking on the link to view the book's item details page. From the item details page, the individual can make the purchase.

Short List It!

Create a "short list" of bestsellers by picking out 3 to 5 titles that approach a concept you would consider writing about. As you study the short list, pay particular attention to the wording of each of the item descriptions and teasers that really catch your attention. Are you drawn in by an interesting cover graphic? Great titles and cover art are important for all books, but with ebooks, it's not so much the cover that sells the book; it's the title, subtitle and the item description. Keep this in mind as you write your content. What will be the perfect title and a great description for your content that will hook readers in and make them want to read the entire book? Which section of text will you offer for your readers to sample? You will want to strive to make sure your titling and promotional text leave the reader craving more!

Dig Deeper

Don't stop at just looking at the titles, subtitles and descriptions of your short-listed bestsellers, though. Amazon provides a wealth of information that will kick your efforts into high gear, including sample texts for digital books. When you come across an intriguing title, download and read the sample. If you don't have a Kindle device, not a problem. Just download the free Kindle app for your iPhone or iPad from iTunes, or obtain the app from Google Play for Android devices. You can also read sample texts from your Amazon account on a computer. A browser-based Kindle reader will launch when you opt to read Amazon Cloud content from your computer. When you "purchase" the sample text, the sample is automatically saved to your Amazon Cloud account.

Just a side note about reading content written by other authors: Reading books by authors I admire stimulates me more than anything else I can do to enhance my motivation. If the author's writing is poor, I am constantly "improving" on his content as I read. If the author's writing is excellent, I absorb the quality of writing like a sponge, attempting to determine exactly what makes the words so compelling. I always take the opportunity to learn from other authors. After all, we can ALL improve our skills.

Read the reviews for the titles on your short list. What do readers say about the content? The writing? Take note of reviews with 3, 4 and 5 stars. (One-star reviews are often written by individuals who despise everything. That is, unless the book received a slew of 1-star reviews. Then you should probably take heed. Apparently, most readers who purchased the book are not happy campers.) Make an effort to incorporate the reviewers' useful and constructive critiques into your future writing. After all, the reader is your customer. Do whatever it takes to make your customer happy.

Reddit

Reddit is a news and entertainment social network where users can post content and links to just about any topic under the sun. Reddit's slogan claims that the network is the "front page of the Internet." I don't know about all that, but I do know that Reddit is HOT. The platform is very popular with millennials, so if this is your target audience, do yourself a favor and spend a few hours perusing Reddit for ideas. You'll find a steady stream of trending topics on this site.

Other Sources of Inspiration

I'm an avid Twitter user so when I am weighing my options for book topics, I simply ask my followers for their input. People who follow you on Twitter are usually more than happy to brainstorm for you when you need it. At least this is the case with my followers. If you are a Facebook user, create a poll and ask your friends to respond. Ask for additional input from the most trusted friends in your FB crew. Try to keep the conversation at a high level so you don't get bogged down in details, though. For me, that's the quickest way to sap my motivation and turn the entire effort into a Netflix binge-watching session. Keep it light and easy, and consider all options presented to you.

Generating Your Concept

By now, you have spent a few hours with the Amazon Bestsellers and Reddit, and maybe you have polled your Facebook friends and Twitter followers for ideas. You should now have an idea of what topics are trending with ebook readers and what subjects interest your circle of friends. Hopefully, during the journey, ideas have begun to percolate and your motivation has started to spring forth.

What's Your Angle?

If you are anything like me, once ideas start to spark during the conceptual phase, they tend to flow one after the other. Jot down potential titles and topics, then select the one that most interests you. After studying the titles and subtitles of a few of the bestsellers, you should now have an idea of the content that is available in your genre of interest. Now, it's simply a matter of determining what's missing in the current body of work, and then moving toward the goal of filling that void.

Roughing It Out

By now, your creative juices should be flowing and you should have an idea of your topic and angle. Start writing by first creating a rough outline of the topic you want to explore. My rough draft for this book was just a rough sketch of 5 to 6 chapters. I say "5 to 6" because I don't try to structure my rough outlines. I just brainstorm how I see the topic materializing on the page. Once I have the gist of what I plan to cover, I then start the process of organizing the chunks of information into chapters.

Many writers first divide their rough outlines into sections, and then chapters, or vice versa. To be honest, I don't like using sections. I don't like reading books that are divided into sections. Quite often, sections feel contrived to me. I prefer to organize my content into chapters that proceed in a logically linear fashion. That's just how I roll. But you can do what works best for you! Ain't America great like that?

To Outsource or Not To Outsource?

That is the question. Do you have the time, energy and discipline to stick with your writing schedule in order to meet your publishing goals? If you are one of the many who just cannot wedge more work into their busy daily routine, consider farming out the project to a freelance writer. Outsourcing your projects is allowed! Yes, it is! You may have never considered doing such a thing until now, but trust me on this one, you can probably afford a ghostwriter who will give her all to bring your book to fruition. Why would you trust me on this, you ask? Well, I spent more than 10 years ghostwriting for other authors. Several of my works are published – under the name of the person who paid me to write them.

Farming It Out

Ghostwriters charge practically nothing for their services. You can probably find a ghostwriter with a Master's degree in English who will charge you $5 or less per single-spaced page. This is the sad reality because there are SO many freelance writers out there, all competing for the same jobs. Finding freelance writers is not a problem, either. Sites like Upwork.com (formerly Elance.com) match contract workers with people looking for freelancers to take on just about any task. Just create an account and post your project. Freelancers will bid on your project and you can follow up by evaluating them based on their profiles and project references. Easy Peasy!

Reputable freelance sites like Freelancer.com and Upwork.com have escrow payment systems in place that protect both the worker and the hiring individual/company, so you don't need to worry about getting ripped off. It's all pretty trustworthy and above board. I've never had a single bad experience on either site, and I've been an Elance member since the service launched in the early 2000's.

Once you have found the winning freelancer and you have had a chance to vet him, initiate a phone call or a Skype interview with the candidate. Freelancers generally work alone and can be solitary to a fault. Though you can conduct your entire project communicating via the site's messaging system, a phone call or video chat kicks off the project and makes it real for all parties involved. Establish a personal connection with the freelancer you select and he will feel like he's got some skin in the game. He will want to do the project for reasons greater than money. He will want to be a part of bringing your passion to reality because you have connected with him. Unicorns and butterflies aside, be sure to have him sign a non-disclosure agreement before you officially hire him for the project.

Image courtesy of Business-Opporunities.biz

Managing Your Project

Ah, my specialty! I'm a Project Management Professional, aka a PMP, certified by the official PMI organization - so I know a thing or two about managing projects. I've managed several huge federal and state software development projects (not the Obamacare site, though. I swear…) and I can write for days about project management. Most of the information I download, however, would be useless to a writer managing production of his own book.

For our purposes, I can break project management success down into two variables: Organization and Communication. Before you sit down to write in earnest, or before you get your ghostwriter started writing, have a solid idea of your topic, your angle and the overall gist of what you want to say with your book. As a former ghostwriter, I can tell you that there is nothing more frustrating for a freelancer than working for an author who is flying by the seat of his pants. Ghostwriters DO NOT like guesswork. The more specific you can be, the better the project will go. If you are writing on your own, organization is definitely your friend. Being well organized will save you on those days when you just don't feel like putting in your scheduled time.

Organizing Your Project

Project managers organize projects around a calendar. Just a quick FYI: Microsoft Project is just one big giant calendar application with a bunch of fancy graphs like Gantt charts, resource distributions, etc. Ya know, it's hard out here for a PMP… Anyway….

Before we take on a job, project managers must know the timeline for the project. The calendar method is also a great strategy for managing your book project. Print out a calendar from one of many Word calendar templates offered free of charge at the Office.com site.

Identify the drop-dead publishing date for your project and note it on the calendar. Now, assess the time between today and the date you have selected for completion of your goal.

Mark a few milestones between now and your drop-dead date, and then identify a sub-goal for each milestone. If you are flying solo, identify milestones you can celebrate when you successfully reach them. My milestones are generally pretty simple when I'm working alone. I simply split the project timeline into 4 quarters, and then identify what I will have done by each date. If you intend to work with a ghostwriter, plan these milestones around sub-goals of chapters or sections.

Communicating With Your Freelancer

Remember those speech classes you took back in junior high and high school? Remember learning about communication? Well, you can dust off those skills and put them into action for managing your project. Communication is not about what you say, it's about what your audience hears. What is the best way to be heard? Be very clear about the message you want to communicate. The best way for me to effectively communicate in a professional situation is to outline everything I want to cover, and then walk through the meeting in my mind prior to showtime. During the meeting, I use the outline as a checklist to ensure that I've covered all information.

When you communicate with your freelancer, be very clear. Don't leave anything to chance or to the imagination. By attempting to be concrete, you are forced to further organize and solidify your ideas. Also, your freelancer will enjoy clear, concise instructions for reaching the ultimate goal. All she wants from you, besides the obvious "getting paid" thing, is to make you happy. Give her a chance to do this by clearly communicating your ideas and goals.

Going It Alone

Discipline is a mindset that begins with the "quality decision." Just like taking on a monumental task of losing a great deal of weight or quitting smoking, you absolutely MUST make a quality decision that you ARE going to do this and you WILL reach the goal of publishing this book. No ifs, ands or buts about it. Once you make up your mind that this is how it's going to be and that's all there is to it, your subconscious mind gets in line with your steel will to help you reach that goal. If you subscribe to the theory of the Law of Attraction, you could posit that making that key quality decision turns on the LOA vibes. No matter how you explain it, making that quality decision – or as I like to say, getting just pissed off enough to do something about it – is essential for your success.

Making Time

Now that you are on your way with your topic, it is time to establish a writing schedule. I advise to commit yourself to at least 5 days per week, 5 hours per day for project work. If you are like me, that 5 hours will easily morph into 10 when you're on a roll. Be sure to schedule 2 full days off from writing, if you can afford the luxury. Your brain needs to reset. You will find that staying well rested makes you more productive. Sure, you can get away with a few midnight sessions, but overall, you need to take your sleep and relaxation seriously because your creativity – and your health - depends on it.

Try your schedule out for a week or two. If you find that you can't keep up, revisit the idea of farming out the work to a freelancer. You may be able to farm out certain sections while you work on others. The key to partnering up with a ghostwriter is organization. If you have set a clear course with your outline, the battle is all but won.

Such a Tool

After many years of using open source word processing applications like OpenOffice and Abiword, I finally relented and obtained a copy of MS Word when the Kindle platform began to favor the Microsoft product for manuscript submissions. The KDP is now tightly integrated with Microsoft Word. You can either upload your final manuscript as a PDF, as a Word document (.docx format) or as a Word HTML package. For best results, Amazon recommends the latter option. To maintain table and image formatting, save your complete manuscript as a filtered web page file (.htm, .html) in Word. When using CreateSpace, you can upload your manuscript as a Word document or a PDF. In any case, do yourself a favor and use Word for your content. More about the technical details of using CreateSpace later in the book. For now, just make sure that you have the tools you need installed on your computer before you sit down to write.

So by now, all of your prep work is finished and you are ready to sit down and start writing. You've probably been mulling your introduction and a few chapters without even trying. It's time to make it all happen...

Tamar Clevenger

CHAPTER 3: WRITING YOUR MONEYMAKER

Now that you have a rough draft of your outline, and you've had some time to think about your topic, start fleshing out the outline and filling in the blanks. Your chapters should now be taking shape. A word about chapters: Make sure each chapter is a standalone entity. Each chapter should have an introduction, middle and a conclusion. By viewing each chapter as a standalone piece, you can farm out sections should you find yourself overwhelmed during the project.

Just Do It!

Tackle the chapter that you find most interesting first. Once you start writing, the ideas will flow naturally. Just don't go for more than a couple of days without writing at least a few paragraphs. You quickly lose that momentum and your train of thought can easily derail. Taking a day or two off while continuing to ponder your project, however, will energize you and revive your creativity.

Continue to learn from the masters while you work. I take a break at least once per day to read a chapter or article written by one of my many favorite authors. You will find words! What I mean by this is that, while you write, you tend to get tunneled into using your tried and true expressions. By exposing yourself to the writings of other authors, your brain picks up on pertinent words and phrases you can use in your own writing. Symbiosis is a beautiful thing!

Back That Thing Up

One final piece of advice: Back up your work every single day. Create a free, throw-away email account on Gmail or Hotmail so you can have a place to upload your work that doesn't rely on your computer or home network. I've experienced so many mysterious occurrences that have caused me to lose work, from computer hard drives melting down to cloud services that just go out of business while hosting all my data. I generally back up my work using 2 or 3 different methods. I email a copy of my manuscript to myself each day – sending the email from my actual email account to my throw-away freebie account. I also save my work each day to a thumb drive. Oh, and did I mention that I keep several copies on my hard drive just in case one gets corrupted. Yes, I know it's a huge pain in the tuchas, but I can tell you from experience, the alternative of losing all your work sucks even harder.

Image courtesy of SodaHead.com

Now, do your thang! Write that compelling content! I'll meet you at CreateSpace when you're finished.

Tamar Clevenger

CHAPTER 4: MASTERING CREATESPACE

Congratulations on making it to CreateSpace! You are a most awesome author, completing your book and all.

The time has finally come to get your work on the CreateSpace platform and pull the trigger to publish your book. The first order of business is to create an account on CreateSpace.com and provide your tax and financial information for receiving your royalty payments. Amazon will need to verify your bank account which takes a few days, so do this as soon as you create your account to get the ball rolling.

Your CreateSpace Account

When you log into the CreateSpace platform after you have initially set up your account, you will see your Member Dashboard. You can manage your publications, account, profile and other tasks from this dashboard.

However, you are probably ready to go ahead and get started on the publishing process for your new book.

The Publishing Process

So you've made it this far and now you're ready to publish your work. From here on out, you will work primarily on the CreateSpace platform to get your book in shape and accepted by Amazon staff. The process occurs in 3 stages: The first stage involves selecting the title, subtitle, description and any other information that will be stated in the Amazon listing of your book. During the second stage, you will sculpt your manuscript into a form that will be converted into both a paperback and an ebook. The third stage is devoted to creating your front and back covers. Amazon does offer some help in case you get stuck at any point during the publishing process. Once you have published your masterpiece, we cover how to market your work to generate income.

CreateSpace Assistance

Amazon provides a few tools to assist you in the publishing process, including the Interior Reviewer and the Cover Creator. The Interior Reviewer checks your manuscript to ensure that it is in a compatible format, and you can use the Cover Creator to quickly create a generic cover in a matter of minutes.

However, If you need more help than the tools can provide, the CreateSpace professional editorial staff will answer brief questions. If you need more help than just the answer to a passing question or two, CreateSpace offers paid professional publishing assistance to authors. To request a free consultation to learn more about CreateSpace's fee-based services, complete the information on their Contact page. The CreateSpace experts can help you with tasks like:

- Editing

- Interior Layout

- Cover Design

- Custom Publishing Solutions

Title and Author Information

The first order of business is to initiate a new listing for your book. Log into the CreateSpace platform, and then click the "Add New Title" option at the top of the page or in the left sidebar. The Add New Title form opens. Enter the title of your book in the "Tell Us The Name Of Your Project" field. Note that you can change the title any time before final submission.

Next, select the "Paperback" radio button. Note that there is no option for a Kindle-only publication. However, when you select the Paperback option, you can offer your book as a Kindle ebook without any additional work. Finally, click the "Get Started" button next to the Guided option. The Guided option provides you with a step-by-step tutorial as you enter the required data. If you published on CreateSpace before, you can select the "Expert" option to enter all relevant information on one long form without specific instructions.

When you click the "Get Started" button, the next page you see will be the details page for your listing. The title field will be filled in with the title you inserted in the previous step. Now, type in your subtitle and complete the author and contributor fields. Select the date that you will publish the project, if you have a specific date in mind. Otherwise, leave the Publication Date field blank, and then click "Save" to save the page or click "Save and Continue" to continue on to the next step. If you do not enter a date, the date that your listing is approved for Amazon will be posted as your official publishing date.

The ISBN

All published works must have an ISBN number. CreateSpace is kind enough to provide a generic ISBN number for your book free of charge! However, you also have the option to create a custom ISBN for a small charge. If you have purchased an ISBN from Bowker or a similar agency, you can use this number instead of obtaining one through Amazon. Select your ISBN preference, and then proceed to the next step. If you select the free CreateSpace option, your ISBN is automatically generated and assigned for your book. You can find your book's ISBN at any time by clicking on the book's title from your CreateSpace dashboard, and checking the top of the left sidebar. Once the ISBN is assigned, you can always find it in the book's listing.

Formatting Your Bestseller

Book Interior

After you have finalized your ISBN, you will see the Book Interior page on the CreateSpace platform. On this page, you will need to specify whether your book will be printed in black and white or color. If you have pictures, select color. Otherwise, save the bandwidth and select the black and white option.

Choose the size of your book in the Trim Size section. I prefer to use the 6x9 option; however, CreateSpace offers several industry-standard sizes from which you can choose. You can also select a non-standard template from this page. After you have selected your book size, download the corresponding Word template (Note the download link below the Trim Size options box). You will use this template to create your front and back matter, and format your manuscript text into the book's complete interior.

Notice that the CreateSpace app keeps track of your progress throughout the publishing process by documenting the steps you have completed, as well as those you have yet to finish, in the left sidebar of the dashboard. You can save your work on the platform, and then return at a later time to complete the process. Just log back into the dashboard, and then click the place where you left off in the sidebar. You're right back in the mix! I bring this up now because, as you have probably already surmised, it's time to leave the CreateSpace platform for a short while and focus on formatting and finalizing your content.

Formatting for Kindle

- Table of Contents

If you intend to offer your book as a Kindle ebook, one important factor to remember is that page numbers are not as critical on a mobile device as they are for a paperback or hard cover books. Readers tend to navigate ebooks using the Table of Contents and bookmarks instead of page numbers. For this reason, you need to make sure that you have correctly formatted your Word document's table of contents to ensure successful Kindle conversion.

If you are using Word on a PC, check out Microsoft's instructions for developing an active table of contents. If you are using Word on a Mac, you'll need to manually create your table of contents using hyperlinks and bookmark anchors to connect to your content. Create your table of contents before plugging your manuscript into the downloaded template.

- Front Matter

Now, it is time to start the process of integrating your manuscript into the template. Start by creating the front matter section directly inside the template. You will then insert your existing manuscript into the template after the front matter pieces.

The front matter of your book includes, at a minimum, a title page. You can also include a dedication page, a copyright section, a preface and a prologue if you so desire. Your title page should be centered on the page, with the title line prominently presented. The author's name should appear under the title in slightly smaller font, also centered. Finally, add a manual page break after the author's name line.

If you include a copyright section, this page usually follows immediately after the title page. Next, the dedication is inserted, then the preface, and finally the prologue. Insert a manual page break after each section. You are now ready to integrate your manuscript text into the template.

- Interior Content

Simply select all text in your manuscript, and then copy and paste the text into the template. You will need to manually insert a page break at the end of the final sentence in each chapter to ensure the next chapter starts at the top of the following page. Organize and index your images. Clean up any stray text and finalize formatting for all pictures, inserts and tables. Double-check your Table of Contents and proofread the manuscript one more time once all text is placed in the template to ensure everything transferred property.

- Back Matter

Now that your content resides in the template, it is time to create the back matter for your book. Back matter consists of appendices, a bibliography, a glossary and any notes that you want to include to direct your reader to more information. If you are including any of the back matter items, chances are you have already written them along with your manuscript. If not, though, now is the time to finalize this section.

If you need more information about formatting your book for publishing on the platform, check out this comprehensive CreateSpace step-by-step guide.

Covering Your Cover

You may not be able to tell a book by its cover, but an interesting cover will attract more readers than a boring one. On the CreateSpace platform, you have three options for generating a cover for your book. You can create your own cover, save it as a PDF file, and then upload it to CreateSpace – OR – you can use the free Cover Creator app. If you want to create your own PDF cover, take a look at the specifications you must consider on this CreateSpace help page. The third option is to outsource your cover. CreateSpace offers the services of illustrators and designers who will create a custom cover for a fee.

To create your cover, log into your CreateSpace dashboard, and then click the "Cover" link in the left sidebar. Even if you haven't yet uploaded your interior content, you can skip to the Cover section to design your cover without losing your place in the publishing process.

First, choose whether the paperback copy of your book will have a matte or glossy cover. If you intend to hire a CreateSpace pro to design your cover, select the "Professional Cover Design" option. If you have a custom cover saved in PDF format ready to go, click the "Upload a Print-Ready PDF" option, and then upload your custom PDF.

To launch the Cover Creator app and create your own cover, click the "Build Your Cover Online" radio button. When you select this option, the Flash Cover Creator app launches. First, select a theme for your cover. Your title and author information will automatically populate in the correct fields. Click the "Front Cover Image" link in the left sidebar, and then select an image for your cover. Click "Next" or select the "Back Cover Text" in the left sidebar.

Type the text that will appear on the back cover in the appropriate section. One **VERY IMPORTANT** note: Take a great deal of care writing the back cover text because this text will become the description for your book in the Amazon listing for your paperback! This fact is not obvious during the publishing process, nor is it noted anywhere in the Cover Creator app. You're welcome!

If you don't like the defaults, you can change the background and font colors by selecting these options in the left sidebar. When finished designing the cover, click the "Submit Cover" button. That's it! You can edit your cover any time prior to final submission for publication.

For more information about using the Cover Creator app, check out the CreateSpace article, How to Make a Basic Cover or download the Cover Creator video tutorial.

Farming Out Your Cover

Your cover design is another element you can outsource for a small fee. Sites like Damonza.com and AuthorSupport.com match writers with experienced book cover designers. The price for professional book cover creation on these sites can range from $50 to over $500.

Crowdsourcing sites like 99Designs.com, Freelancer.com and Upwork.com enable you to post your project and have professional designers bid on the work. If you want to take the discount route, sites like Fiverr.com provide a platform for matching designers (and other contract workers) with individuals and companies in need of their services. Fiverr's claim to fame is the jobs on the site are offered for very low prices, generally $5.

Completing the Publishing Process

The final step before submitting your book for publishing is to review all of the CreateSpace steps. If you click the "Complete Setup" link in the left sidebar, you will be taken to a review page that shows all sections on one page – each section contains an Edit button. Review all sections and clean up any typos, strange formatting and poorly worded text. You are now ready to submit for publishing.

When you submit for publishing, the platform will automatically check several items; however, your book must also endure a final review by CreateSpace staff. Don't worry, though! They will not be editing or critiquing your content in any way. What the CreateSpace team will be looking for is bad formatting and technical issues that will cause problems when the book is printed, such as text that bleeds into the margins. You will receive an email within 24 hours detailing the remaining steps you need to take to comply with the formatting rules. In most cases, these changes are very minor. Make the required changes and resubmit your book. While you wait for the notification that your book has been published and is live on the Amazon platform, check out the Marketing Your Bestseller section and start marketing your book.

Pricing Strategies

The pricing of your book is an important factor. Study the pricing of similar books in your genre and price accordingly. For Kindle books, Amazon pro writers suggest that the sweet spot for a book like the one you are reading resides around the $2.99 mark. I tend to offer my books for a slightly lower price, but some authors of similar works will go as low as $.99. You will need to decide two pricing strategies: One for the paperback and 1 one for the Kindle ebook. Review KDP pricing specials, such as Kindle Unlimited and KDP Direct. Participate in these programs to enhance your sales.

The Kindle platform offers two royalty levels for authors: 70% and 35%. You maintain much more pricing flexibility when you choose the 35% option. Additionally, the 70% option is not offered in all locales. To select the 70% option, your ebook must by priced 20% lower or more than your print copy. Research these two royalty levels and determine which level works best for your creation.

CreateSpace vs. KDP

I wrote this book about publishing via the CreateSpace platform because CreateSpace will publish your book as a paperback and as a Kindle ebook at the same time. CreateSpace automatically publishes your book to Kindle Direct when you select this option during the publishing process. However, you can bypass the hard copy publishing process and publish your work solely as a digital piece using the Kindle Direct Publishing (KDP) platform.

Log into KDP using your CreateSpace or Amazon credentials. Save your completed manuscript as a filtered web page in Word (.htm, .html), and then upload your formatted content to the KDP platform. Upload a cover and publish your ebook for the entire world to see! The process takes just a few minutes to submit and your ebook is available on the Amazon Kindle store site within about 12 hours! Note that when you use CreateSpace and you enroll in KDP, your CreateSpace titles will be listed in your KDP bookshelf as the two platforms are tightly integrated.

Note that Kindle ebook files must be 50 Mb or smaller, so compress your manuscript as much as possible before submitting it. Amazon offers a free ebook, "Building Your Book For Kindle," that covers KDP formatting and technical considerations in detail.

CHAPTER 5: MARKETING YOUR BESTSELLER

As a self-published author, you are an entrepreneur and your book is your startup's product. If you think in these terms, marketing your book takes on a whole new perspective. Become your own cheerleader. Be an evangelist for your work. Use all the available online services you can maneuver to promote your book and drive up your sales.

Dedicated Website

Bestselling authors usually create a dedicated website for each new book they are promoting. You can create a website for your title with virtually no technical knowledge and very little effort. Several website hosting services offer users the opportunity to create free websites with drag and drop tools. However, if you want to use a specific domain name, you will need to purchase the name from a domain registrar. Domain names are inexpensive and most website hosting services will set one up for you for a small fee. Use the dedicated website as a landing place for referrals. If you have a site dedicated solely to your book, you always have a place to refer potential readers. Your referrals won't need to wade through a bunch of irrelevant information just to find out more about your book.

Image courtesy of WritersLiving.com

Blog

Start a blog where you can provide updates and additional information about your book's topic as it becomes available. Blogs provide a platform to interact with your readers, and you can even attach a blog to your book's dedicated website. Two birds with one stone. Just make sure you have some time each week to write a few blog posts. If you don't have time to create and maintain your own blog, write a few guest posts for other writer blogs. You can always add a link to your book's site in your byline.

Social Media

If you are not already on social media, now is a good time to get involved. I you are an active Facebook user in your personal life, you may have never though considered the platform as a marketing tool. Facebook is an excellent way to spread the word about your new book. Twitter is another great tool. You can keep your marketing efforts separate from your personal activities by creating Facebook pages and Twitter accounts devoted entirely to promoting your product. You can even create a stand-along Facebook fan page for your book promotions. Promote your page and author accounts on your personal social media sites to drive up your sales.

Author Profiles

Create an author profile to spread the word about your new release to other authors and potential readers. Amazon hosts a platform for authors to create and manage profiles. The author profile gives the writer web space to provide readers with additional information, such as an extended bio. Check out NY Times bestselling author Tim Ferriss' author profile on Amazon for ideas for establishing your own author identity. Another site that allows authors to post detailed profiles is Goodreads.com.

Reviews

One way to propel you book into high sales is to obtain glowing reader reviews. When you first start out, you can leverage your friends, family, Facebook acquaintances and Twitter followers to review your book. Some authors resort to purchasing positive reviews. This practice is discouraged, mainly because torrid details like this tend to eventually come out. Just think! One day, you may be a famous bestselling author.

The last thing you want is a scandal about how you bought good reviews early in your career.

ABE: Always Be Evangelizing

Remember the catch phrase from "Glengarry Glenn Ross"? "ABC: Always Be Closing." Regardless of the channels you choose for promoting your work, always be in the process of evangelize for your book. Visit blogs that post information in your niche, and then offer readers sample text from your book in guest posts and comments. Answer questions within the areas of your expertise on the Quora site, and accompany your answers with a link to your book. Continue to mention your book to social media friends and followers – without beating it into the ground, of course. Get the word out using every opportunity you find.

Explore unconventional methods of evangelizing for your book, too. If you can create a buzz, who knows?! You may have a viral bestseller on your hands! Good luck with your efforts!

CHAPTER 6: CONCLUSION

Our journey is now coming to an end. To quote the infamous Jerry Garcia, What a long, strange trip it's been! We've been through so much over the course of this journey, I feel like I can now share a secret with you. I'm not sure if the secret will motivate you or simply piss you off, but here goes!

There is a saying in the world of software development: "Eat Your Own Dogfood." This means that we strive to design software that we would use, and then once it is developed, we use it. The same concept applies to the writing of this book. I have published on both CreateSpace and KDP prior to writing this work, but this time, I documented every step of the process. I ate my own dogfood and used the process I documented here to complete and publish this very book. This book is proof positive that the system is successful.

Now, here comes the part that might cause you a little discomfort. I wrote this book from start to finish, finalized and published it - all in the span of 5 days. My timeline was literally only 5 days! I put off this project for about 3 years and now that I look back, I can see how foolish I was for procrastinating so long. I hope you can take a lesson from my experience and make a vow to yourself to get to work right away.

The breakdown of my timeline for this book:

Day 1: I brainstormed for a concept, identified an idea and created a rough draft. I also installed Word on my computer and got my office set up for some serious work.

Day 2: I continued to research the bestsellers, reading samples and reviews. I then fleshed out the outline and wrote Chapter 1.

Day 3: I wrote Chapters 2 and 3, created the Table of Contents and blocked out headings for the entire document.

Day 4: I wrote Chapters 4, 5 and 6, started the CreateSpace listing and created the cover.

Day 5: I plugged my content into the CreateSpace template, proofread the entire document, finalized formatting and submitted the final work for CreateSpace review.

Marketing is an ongoing effort, so this task is not included in my timeline.

So now that you know about the history of this book, you really have no excuses. Granted, this is a brief how-to book that addresses a finite process. However, creating the timeline and schedule for your project follows the same logical steps. The process documented in this book WORKS – and the book itself is proof positive. So, get busy! The world awaits your contribution. Good luck!

Tamar Clevenger

ABOUT THE AUTHOR

Tamar Clevenger holds a Master's degree from University of Illinois at Chicago. She is also a certified Project Management Professional (PMP) with over 20 years' experience managing large, high profile software development projects for federal, state and municipal agencies.

As a ghostwriter, Ms. Clevenger has availed her talents to various authors and bloggers to successfully publish over 5,000 articles and posts over the past 10 years.

Tamar Clevenger

www.ingramcontent.com/pod-product-compliance
Lightning Source LLC
Chambersburg PA
CBHW040315010626
45792CB00022B/333